Reduce the Number and Size of Governments

Reduce Administrative Costs

Tom, the Twenty-First-Century Radical

iUniverse, Inc.
Bloomington

Reduce the Number and Size of Governments
Reduce Administrative Costs

iUniverse books may be ordered through booksellers or by contacting:

iUniverse
1663 Liberty Drive
Bloomington, IN 47403
www.iuniverse.com
1-800-Authors (1-800-288-4677)

Because of the dynamic nature of the Internet, any web addresses or links contained in this book may have changed since publication and may no longer be valid. The views expressed in this work are solely those of the author and do not necessarily reflect the views of the publisher, and the publisher hereby disclaims any responsibility for them.

Any people depicted in stock imagery provided by Thinkstock are models, and such images are being used for illustrative purposes only.

Certain stock imagery © Thinkstock.

ISBN: 978-1-4620-2244-1 (sc)
ISBN: 978-1-4620-2245-8 (e)

Printed in the United States of America

iUniverse rev. date: 07/05/2011

TABLE OF CONTENTS

AUTHOR'S NOTE

The author has studied the relationship between corporate organization and effective decision making. Governments have not followed the procedures used by corporations to manage budget problems. As a result, we have excessive governments that are inefficient and dysfunctional.

As one reads this book, it will appear that the author is attempting to reorganize governments. The intention of the author is to provide data and ideas that support a collective search for wisdom to improve governments at all levels. The merger of local and county governments will reduce administrative costs. In regard to the federal government, the book supports the need for a constitutional convention charged with improving the effectiveness and the efficiency of the federal government.

The data and information contained in this book is available to everyone. The author has relied on Internet search engines to confirm the facts that support the conclusions. The *Rand McNally Yearly Road Atlas 2011* is another excellent source for data, such as number of counties in a state, as well as the number of metropolitan areas, towns, and villages.

There are slight differences in population and other data derived from the Internet, but these differences are not sufficient to change the conclusions. As we have learned from the census, counting population is not an exact science.

ACKNOWLEDGMENTS

The author thanks his wife, Eunice, for putting up with him for sixty-six years. A very special thanks, as always, to the publishers. Without their help, it would never have been possible to complete this book.

FOREWORD

This book is a sequel to—or a second edition of—the book titled *Save Tax Dollars*. The author has learned many things as a result of the publication of that book. This book contains much of that knowledge and provides additional data to support the suggestions and conclusions of both books.

Some of the statements and suggestions made in this book will seem to be very radical to some readers. The call for reduction of Congress and the executive branch, and the suggested mergers of state, county, and local governments are radical. Radicals think outside of the box. They attempt to avoid false barriers to their decision-making process.

It is time for a collective search for wisdom to improve the governments at all levels. Citizens should utilize their sovereign rights and bring about improvements in all governments. Our governments are "of the people, by the people, for the people." While the freedoms granted by the Constitution are timeless, the organization and methods of government are time dependent.

Three things are desirable before you plan for the future:

(1) It is good to know where you are, (2) it is necessary to look into the past and learn how you got to the present status quo, and (3) a collective search for wisdom is the best approach for committees, boards, councils, and legislatures to solve a problem or make a decision.

CHAPTER 1
WHAT IS THE STATUS QUO?

The population of the earth and the nation grow at an exponential rate. Populations grow like compound interest, multiplying the amount by some percentage at regular intervals. At any time, the rate of growth is proportional to the size already achieved. All governments need to take population growth into consideration before any action or decision.

When population growth is not taken into account, actions and decisions have a short life. Population growth was important in the 18th century and the early 1800s, when the federal government was formed. In the twenty-first century, there is a much larger rate of growth. This makes the population factor much more important.

When the Constitution was written, the population was just over one million citizens. Today, there are more than three hundred million citizens. Both personal freedom and individual sovereignty—granted by the Constitution—are timeless, but government's decisions depend on time and population.

Today, the country is witnessing the results of this lack

of concern for population growth. The Constitution did not address this issue. The population and the rate of growth of the population were not factors in consideration for statehood or the formation of county and municipal governments.

While the tax base increases as the population grows, the cost of services increases proportionally. Therefore, population and tax bases are very important factors for all governments. Careful control of administrative costs is necessary to prevent excessive overhead spending.

When the framers of the Constitution decided on a bicameral Congress, their lack of concern for population growth resulted in a large, excessive, and inefficient federal Congress. It was not until the Congress of 1913 that it was realized that changes in the government were needed. There was an attempt to correct the mistakes of the writers of the Constitution. The number of seats in the House of Representatives was set at 435.

Before this action was taken, the growth of the House of Representatives was proportional to the population growth. As a result of this action in 1913, every ten years, there is an increase in the population that a House of Representative member represents.

The delays in action from the 1800s until 1913 allowed an overgrowth of the federal Congress. The number of members in the House of Representatives grew from 30 to 435 in 1913. The 1913 Congress might have realized that 435 was an excessive number of members. They could have reduced the membership to at least one half the 435. If the Senate operates with one hundred members, why does it take 435 members of the House? One hundred members in the Senate could represent the States and one hundred members in the House could represent the people.The question needs to be asked: Do we need a bicameral

Congress? Another action of this Congress changed the manner in which senators were elected. Before 1913, senators were appointed by the state legislature.

While more than 130 years elapsed before Congress decided to improve the government, the changes were minimal. The changes did stop the growth of the House of Representatives, but did nothing to reduce the overgrowth of Congress that had occurred over this long period.

Now that the Constitution is over one hundred years older, it is time for major changes in the Constitution for the twenty-first century. One thing that has not changed is the statement in the Declaration of Independence that says, "That whenever any form of government becomes destructive of these ends, it is the right of the people to alter or to abolish it, and to institute new government, laying its foundation on such principles and organizing its powers in such form, as to them shall seem most likely to effect their safety and happiness."

A federal Congress of 535 members results in excessive administrative costs and contributes to the difficulty in decision making. Why does it take 435 House members to cover the work done by one hundred senators? Why does the same work have to be done by two houses of Congress? Both houses hold costly conferences, hearings, and debates on the same subjects. Fewer members of Congress means less pork in the budget.

Many government actions and decisions happen after a major time period has elapsed. This delay before any action is taken results in major problems and complicates the decision process. The bicameral Congress requires long time periods for decision-making.

When actions and decisions are time dependent, it is necessary to stay in touch with the results of the action or decision. A timely correction in the action or decision improves efficiency. The two-party system and the 535 members of the bicameral Congress are the major causes of delayed decisions.

Many times, decision-making problems are caused by a separation between the decision makers and the individuals affected by the decision. During the nation's formative years, information was disseminated at a very slow rate. The advances in electronics and media coverage have corrected part of this problem. The nation's increased population and more than three million square miles of area cause a major separation between the decision-makers and those affected by the decisions.

Most often, two mistakes are made by decision makers: (1) the decision is made without adequate consideration of affects the decision may have, or (2) the decision is made without sufficient consideration of all the factors that are necessary to make a proper decision. Of the two problems, the first has the greatest adverse effect.

It is very difficult to make decisions today that are common to all parts of the nation. There are many differences between the populations, industries, and resources of the states.

STATE SOVEREIGNTY

While some articles and amendments to the Constitution are ambiguous, the Tenth Amendment is not. The amendment states, "The powers not delegated to the United States by the Constitution, nor prohibited by it to the states, <u>are reserved to the states respectively</u>, or to the people." It is clear that the federal government's powers are limited to powers granted by the Constitution. The remaining powers, not forbidden by the Constitution, belong to the states or the people.

The federal government overgrowth has taken over many

functions that would be much better organized and have greater efficiency if they were state functions. These functions will be discussed in detail in future chapters. Clearly, many actions of the federal Congress are not among the powers granted the Congress by the Constitution.

As in the past, several states are currently claiming their states' rights granted by the Tenth Amendment. Their lawsuits claim decisions made by Congress and the president are unconstitutional. The laws enacted by Congress and the actions of the president have had adverse effects on the budgets of the states. The detrimental effects of their actions have most states in very serious financial conditions. Their budgets are underfunded and they have large, increasing deficits.

The diversity of the fifty states has caused the oversized federal government to be out of touch with the various areas of the country. It is currently difficult for one law to fit all states and situations.

As an example, the Gulf of Mexico oil spill caused the president to ban deep water oil drilling in the gulf. Washington thought that this was a good idea. The oil spill caused massive unemployment. The president's decision resulted in further reduction in employment in Louisiana. The state sued to have the ban overturned because of the adverse effects.

Many of the states were against the stimulus bill because the structure of the bill resulted in increases in the state budget. While the bill provided one-time relief, subsequent budgets were not sufficient to cover the added cost to the states. Once again, time and the tax base were not part of the decision.

Mandated federal government programs have added to state debt. The cost of all programs, federal, state, or local must be covered by the tax base. Carrying out unfunded programs increases the debt. When the federal government mandates a program for the good of the citizens, the federal government should cover the cost of the program with a tax. The federal government requiring the state to fund a federal program appears to be a violation of the Tenth Amendment.

The government's organization and methods lead to dysfunction and inefficiency. This dysfunction and inefficiency cannot be blamed completely on the current federal government. The Constitution and the method of government have not changed as the United States has grown in area and population.

The population growth has led to overgrowth and dysfunction in the federal government, and disorganization in state, county, and local governments. When the federal government devises a program, it should be done under the Tenth Amendment. Before the program is approved, state and individual freedom should be considered.

While the states are engaged in budget-cutting operations, these cuts are largely coming for state employees other than the legislature. Why do states have two houses in the legislature like the federal government? The State leaders should be leaders not followers. One State, Nebraska has shown leadership. Nebraska is the only State that does not have a bicameral legislature. State senators and house members are elected from districts in the state. Reducing the numbers of legislative offices would reduce the budget and improve a collective search for wisdom in problem solving. Administrative cost-savings occur each year after the saving occurs. This is not a one-time saving.

FEDERAL GOVERNMENT PROBLEMS

In 2009, the federal government collected $2.1 trillion in taxes. However, the government spent $3.5 trillion. Thus, the deficit was $1.4 trillion. The taxes collected were $1.4 trillion less than that required to cover the excessive spending of the federal government. The tax base and budget must determine the demands of the government. The Congress and the president stated the debt in terms of a percentage of gross national product. Now the debt is the same as the gross national product. Einstein said it was stupid to keep doing the same thing and expecting a different result. The author does not think anyone can spend themselves into prosperity. It is by knowing the value of money and saving in the good times for expenses in the bad times that prosperity is achieved.

The president's budget deficit projections are different from the Congressional Budget Office's budget deficit projections. In other words, the policy changes embodied in President Obama's 2012 budget put our country deeper in debt. While a figure for the debt is needed, the estimates vary. With the inefficiency in government, exact figures for the budget and the deficit are difficult to obtain. Some of the problems could be related to a planned lack of sunshine in government. Another problem is the time period for the budget effect. Various government agencies use different crystal balls for their projections.

Their projections cause problems with government budgets and deficits. Budget projections frequently occur far out in the future. The members of government say that over the next twenty years there will be a savings of trillions dollars. Does that mean the savings of billions of dollars a year? The answer to this question is no. The savings are projected for many years into the future. Most people do not have the crystal ball that is needed for this kind of projection. Budget planning for one year at a time is necessary. The budget process should be an ongoing process. Changes may be needed during the year.

Increasing debt means increased debt payments. At some point, the debt payment will exceed the government's income. This is bankruptcy. When corporations go bankrupt, they undergo organizational changes. It is better to undergo organizational changes before bankruptcy.

If governments had used corporate methods to reduce their administrative overhead and increase their tax base, governments would not be in debt and the deficit would be manageable. Instead, governments—at all levels—are excessively large and underfunded. The executive administration is constantly asking Congress to increase the debt limit.

Today, the people give Congress a 25 percent approval rating. After a short period in office, presidents have a less than 50 percent approval rating. Therefore, the current government is not "of the people, by the people, for the people." The Declaration of Independence states that the people should organize a government that ensures their "safety and happiness."

FUNDING GOVERNMENT

When corporations reach a size where corporate administration cannot control the company, the company is divided into profit centers. This brings control and decision making nearer to the operations affected by the decisions. The profit center's budget is less than the corporation's budget and can be controlled. Currently, the GAO has difficulty keeping up with government spending.

Governments have forgotten that taxes should only be used to fund the government. Using taxes to bring about social changes is not using taxes to fund government. Tax breaks remove money that is needed to fund the government and complicate the enforcement of tax codes. The loss of funds granted as tax breaks must be obtained from another source. This action moves the tax burden from one tax source to another—or the programs are underfunded and borrowing is necessary to fund the program.

Another major problem with funding governments is the act of robbing Peter to pay Paul. There is a great tendency in both federal and state governments to take funds designated for one purpose and use them for another purpose. At some point, the loss of these funds will make it difficult to fund the robbed program. Taxes need to be assessed to fund each program that is enacted into law at all levels of government. Tax dollars should be collected for a purpose—and tax dollars should not be put in a general or discretionary fund.

The federal government has allowed the tax codes to grow uncontrolled. Spending and the tax base are not balanced. Because of social issues, it is difficult to establish what is considered by all to be a fair tax system.

The current income tax system applies a percentage to the earned income. This percentage increases as income increases. The size of the income determines the rate. Thus, individuals with larger incomes pay taxes at a higher rate.

Yet, our tax codes allow individuals with very large incomes to avoid income taxes. While the oversized Congress and the oversized executive branch argue over trivial problems and politics, major problems like taxes and the budget go without action. Current budgets are underfunded and the deficit increases.

Governments are acting like the population and overusing

credit. Borrowed money must be repaid with added interest. It appears that governments and many people have forgotten that money has value. The Federal Reserve has forgotten that money has value. The Federal Reserve is lending money to banks at zero interest. Thus, banks are paying investors very low interest.

THE ECONOMY

The United States economy is said to be the largest national economy; however, China is near or in first place. The United States Gross Domestic Product was $14 trillion in 2009, which is one-quarter of nominal global Gross National Product - The total value of goods produced and services provided in the United States was one quarter of all Global goods produced and services provided plus the net income from foreign investments. The United States has one-fifth of the total global purchasing power.

Industries in the United States have a major advantage. This nation has the world's most ethnically diverse and multicultural population. This difference provides the United States with a level of marketing ability that other nations do not enjoy.

Even with these advantages, the federal government allowed the development of the recent recession. The Declaration of Independence declared that governments exist for the "safety and happiness" of the people. Despite the high cost of the multilevel organization of our Treasury and Commerce Departments, they failed to protect the "safety and happiness" of the people.

Governments are living on borrowed money. There is an ever-increasing debt. There has been no attempt by Congress— especially the House of Representatives where all money bills start—to reduce the size of the federal government or reduce the spending.

While individual fiat is used by elected members of government to get votes, there is no evidence of a collective search for wisdom to solve the current major economic problems. As a result of recent elections, some members of Congress are attempting to correct this problem.

GROWTH OF THE UNITED STATES

The United States has grown to fifty states spread across 3.54 million square miles. It has a population of more than three hundred million people, but the growth has been disorganized. The population of the fifty states varies from seven states—with less than one million—to California, with a population of more than thirty-six million.

The average state population is near four million. The city of Los Angles alone has a population of almost four million, and the population of New York City is equal to more than twice the average state population. Each state has both county and local governments that vary greatly in population and area. Tax base, as it relates to population, has not been considered in the growth of the nation.

The cost to individual taxpayers varies greatly, depending upon the administrative cost for providing services. The legislatures, councils, and boards set their own number of members, salaries, and office expenses. Taxpayers need to take more interest in how their dollars are spent.

With the large growth in area, population, GNP, and purchasing power, the nation is slowly recovering from a major recession. With our sizable national debt and deficits of the other governments, there is great concern that there will be another, greater recession. There is growing evidence of inflation.

Therefore, the governments of the country have outgrown the government that is required to administer the governed areas. The current size of all governments—federal, state, county, and local—is excessive and requires funding for unnecessary administrative cost.

When one examines the overhead cost by federal government departments, it is obvious that there is a great difference in administrative costs. Medicare and Social Security have very high administrative costs. Despite the very high administrative cost of Medicare, there are frequent reports of Medicare fraud. The inability to organize and operate programs of the oversized federal government is a major cost concern. Similar programs at the state level—where the average population is four million—would be more efficiently and effectively operated.

Social Security is an excellent example of dysfunction and mismanagement. Social Security tax dollars were transferred into the general fund and have been used to support other programs. This is an example of robbing Peter to pay Paul. While many major corporations have annuity programs, it is apparent that these programs were not consulted or considered when Social Security was formed—and are not being considered in order to improve the program.

Social Security was not intended to provide the total income required for retirement. Many factors were overlooked when Social Security became law. The program was to use funds taken from the working population to pay people who were old enough to retire under the program. There was a need for jobs and it was hoped that retirement would provide jobs for the growing population.

In general, this should work because of the rate of growth of the population. However, many factors affected the rate of population growth. After World War II, there was a rapid growth in the population and the GI Bill increased individual income. These economic factors provided salaries large enough to more than adequately support the program.

Now that rapid growth of the population no longer exists— and we have the baby boomer population retiring—the retired population is too large for the working population to support. This funding problem is also complicated by another factor. The lifespan of the population is continually increasing.

Programs should be managed by Congress on a regular basis. Problems like those with Social Security are ignored for long periods. When changes in the program or changes in the tax base are required, they should be made. Accumulating problems cause difficulty in management and decision making. These comments apply to Medicare as well as Social Security. The mismanagement in Medicare is evident in the fraud.

Social Security was enacted into law in 1935. The program was designed for the period. All programs are subject to change over time. But, Congress and the federal administration did not review the program and make the necessary changes as they were required.

The administrative cost of the medical insurance industry is excessive. Better cooperation between physicians' offices and hospitals with the government could substantially reduce overhead. There is a need for a collective search for wisdom at these levels.

While each department and program should have a tax base, there was major discretionary spending in 2010 by the Departments of Health and Human Services, Veteran Affairs,

Education, Housing and Urban Development, and Homeland Security.

With two wars in progress, it is natural that the Veteran Affairs budget would increase. Despite the increased discretionary spending in Housing and Urban Development, many families are losing their homes and the housing market is markedly depressed.

Terrorists have certainly increased the spending of Homeland Security, but many citizens question the effectiveness and efficiency of these discretionary expenses. Discretionary spending by the executive administration is uncontrolled spending—and the spending adds to the budget without a supporting tax base. There should not be a discretionary fund.

States are having difficulty with Medicaid. There is an ever-increasing cost for the program that states claim will bankrupt them. There are many concerns with the so-called Obama health care bill. While the cost of medical care is large, there are other excessive costs. The health insurance industry takes money from direct medical care. The fraud in the program is unbelievable.

Is it time for nationalized medical care? The majority of the citizens have health insurance. These funds would be available as tax income. Direct payments to hospitals and physicians' offices based on average health care costs would substantially reduce fraud. Every day, citizens see ads by medical care companies. Physicians and hospitals need to become more cost conscious and attempt to reduce fraud.

Naturally, every patient is different, but average or median cost covers the patient whose treatment is less expensive—as well as the patient who requires more expensive care.

Hospitals and physicians' offices know what medical

conditions and the number of patients they normally treat over a stated period. These data would assist in government payments. Some diseases may have greatly skewed health care costs. Mean values could be used instead of average values. When unusual cost is involved, it could be made up in the following payment; when excessive payment is made, the funds could be recovered from the next payment.

While the programs could use improvement, many nations now have nationalized health care programs. These programs work with much less administrative costs than the current American programs do—and they provide care to all citizens. With these government programs, a comparison of cost between hospitals and physicians' offices can be made. These comparisons assist in the control of excess cost and fraud.

Naturally, making the suggested changes will take time and preparation. Emergency rooms in cities are overrun with non-emergency patients. The supply of physicians, nurses, and medical assistants will need to be increased—and this requires time. There could be a need for additional hospitals. As with all decisions, thoughtful action is needed before the decision is made.

DATA FROM THE ROAD ATLAS

A look into the *2011 Rand McNally Road Atlas* shows that we have states with less population than many of our cities. The four largest states have populations near or above twenty million. The random nature of the population distribution in cities, villages, towns, counties, and states shows a complete lack of planning for efficiency.

Tax dollars are completely wasted on unnecessary government administration. Frequently, it is obvious that the service requirements are not met by the tax base. In this case, tax dollars from another tax base are being used to support the services of the underfunded governments. Are you paying taxes to support another government area?

From a look at the atlas, it is obvious that many areas and districts with borders and names do not have governments. The services of government are supplied from another place. Society and government are separate functions. This concept will be discussed in detail later in this book.

CHAPTER 2
CURRENT PROBLEMS WITH GOVERNMENTS

Decision making by the oversized federal government does not meet the needs of the entire country. Decisions are made too far from the individuals that are affected by the decision. The British government granted greater sovereignty to parts of the empire. This action kept the empire together for a long time. Granting greater freedoms for self-rule to the states will support national growth, improve decision making, and reduce costs.

When corporations grow to a point where control by the corporate headquarters causes problems, they decentralize and set up profit centers. These profit centers are freestanding parts of the overall corporation. Thus, decision making is nearer to the individual affected and decision making is less complicated.

Spending by the Department of Housing and Urban Development is an excellent example of a need to decentralize government. All development is not urban. Agricultural areas need controlled development. If development was controlled by the local and state areas, decisions would be made closer to the affected areas. Most state, county, and local governments spend money on development more wisely than the federal government does.

Population and land growth has resulted in a remarkable divergence in our country. In addition, sources of energy vary. Some states use hydroelectric, wind, solar, or biofuel for energy. Energy decisions would be better made by the states and not by the Department of Energy.

A reduction in the federal government would greatly reduce the cost of administration. With greater freedom in various parts of the country, laws could be enacted that support local development. With proper organization of the regions, decisions would be made nearer to the individuals affected by the decisions.

CHAPTER 3
HOW DID WE GET TO THE STATUS QUO?

Since the eighteenth century, Americans have always been in charge of their destiny. American citizens have come together to fight adversity. We have seen the American spirit in times of war and peace. States' Rights and individual freedom have remained main concerns of the citizens.

THE FORMATIVE YEARS

The colonists fled persecution and tyranny by European governments. More than one hundred years passed between the first permanent settlement and the consideration of a federal government.

The population and new settlements grew to a population of just over one million by the mid-eighteenth century. The Revolutionary War and the separation from Britain caused a need for organization of a new federal government. The late 1700s and early 1800s were a time of change in the formative years of the United States of America.

The agricultural areas and the frontiersmen were independent survivors and insisted on individual freedom. There was a lasting memory of European persecution and tyranny.

The citizens who lived in the urban industrial areas were more dependent on each other and their society. They tended to be more interested in a strong central government that would increase development and improve world markets. Even in these very early days of the birth of the nation, there were societal differences.

After some resistance, the meeting of the First Continental Congress took place after the British imposed the tax acts caused by the Boston Tea Party. There was little agreement among the members during the First Continental Congress, but the discussion of grievances with King George III clarified the thinking in the colonies. While they were not in agreement on a course of action, the people who attended the Congress became friends.

The Second Continental Congress was the result of New England's battles with the British troops. Thus, the Second Continental Congress managed the war efforts and acted as the central government for the colonies. The Declaration of Independence was drafted during this time, but the Congress had no legal status. The Articles of Confederation was an attempt to form a central government. However, with larger populations wanted a greater say in the Congress and colonies with small populations feared federal government tyranny.

While there was a final agreement by the colonies to the Articles, the Congress remained without the power to tax and had to borrow money. The members of the Congress were trying to fight a war for independence with minimum funds and a growing debt.

The Articles of Confederation had many weaknesses as a method to govern the new United States of America. The Congress formed by the articles called for a convention to draft the Constitution. George Washington was reluctant to attend the Convention, but once present he was elected Chairman. Thomas Jefferson was in France at the time of the Convention. James Madison, a young lawyer from Virginia, was a major force in the Convention. The new Constitution addressed the differences between the states with large populations and the states with smaller populations by establishing a bicameral Congress. The federal government needed the States, but the States, at this time, did not need the Federal Government.

The thirty-six members of Congress were not a concern. The salary was six dollars a day for the time they were in meeting. In the eighteenth century, the bicameral Congress was a reasonable decision to solve a problem. However, it did not take into consideration the fact that the population would increase, resulting in growth and expense of the Congress. It would have been better if the Constitution had created Senate districts instead of House districts. But the need for state support dictated a different decision.

Senators could have been elected by equal population districts rather than having two senators per state. The Constitution should have established a maximum number for the Senate. These decisions would have solved the representation problems for all time—and the senators would have been more responsive to the people.

As a result of the uncontrolled growth of the states and the differences in the state populations, a serious problem has occurred with the one man, one vote concept. The states with small populations control a large percentage of the Senate. The representation in the House does not make up for this difference. The decision to have a bicameral Congress was caused by an interest in having all the states approve the Constitution. Thus, the decision was a result of a problem of the time the decision was made. The concern at the time was for state sovereignty and not individual freedom.

Since the government was a "government of the people, by the people, for the people," it may have been a better decision to have one legislative body—the Senate—elected by districts with equal populations. This decision would have resulted in a correction of the problem for all time. The decision would have been a concession to individual sovereignty in that equal populations would have been represented by a senator. When there is a concern for individual sovereignty, there is greater individual freedom.

Today, there is a major concern about individual freedom caused by the financial conditions of the states. As a result of the states' budget problems, many citizens fear the tyranny of the governor and the legislature.

The freedom of the citizens to form unions and the rights of the unions are in question. Without thought and responsibility for the welfare of society by individuals, everyone suffers the consequences. Individual freedom is important, but individual freedom requires personal responsibility.

Maybe from an unrealized concession to individual freedom, several of the states elected their House members by a vote of all the voters. These states did not develop House districts in the early days of the Constitution. This is another indication that the new states were not giving up their sovereignty to the federal government.

Thomas Paine was born in 1737 and immigrated to the

American Colonies in 1774. He was known as a radical who disseminated messages calculated to assist the cause of freedom from the rule of monarchs. In 1789, he visited France and wrote *The Rights of Man* in support of the French fight against monarchy. *Common Sense* is his best-known work. The pamphlet fueled the debate on independence from the rule of King George III. In 1776, James Charmers wrote *Plain Truth*, supporting British rule and calling Paine a political quack.

James Charmers remained a British loyalist and served as an officer in the First Battalion of the Maryland Loyalists. He was a brilliant military mind and assisted in the capture of Philadelphia. He returned to England after the American Revolution with other expatriates. He continued to publish pamphlets criticizing Paine and his economic policies.

The Declaration of Independence, which was written during these debates, states that, "All men are created equal." This is a statement that birthright does not include the right to rule or govern. This is not a declaration of individual freedom. The power motivation was in operation at this time. The Declaration of Independence did not say that all people are created equal as a politically correct statement would say today. Power motivation always depresses individual freedom.

While the Declaration of Independence is a denial of royal birthrights, the teachings—which have led to the development of the growth of individual freedom that began during the Age of Enlightenment—have not been completely satisfied today.

Individual freedom in the Western world is ahead of the rest of the world. But the female gender still has limits. For example in many cases there is still not equal pay for equal work. Great progress has been made by Western world females, especially in the United States, during the 1900s. Progress is lacking in the

Middle-East and much of the rest of the world. Slavery ended and racial freedom began in the mid-1860s. The Nineteenth Amendment granted women the right to vote in 1920.

While citizens enjoy their freedoms, there is a tendency to neglect the duties of individual freedom. Personal power motivations by the individuals in office have prevented the establishment of individual freedom.

In the eighteenth century, Thomas Paine wrote, "Society in every state is a blessing, but government at its best state is but a necessary evil." He further stated that when government is at its worst state, it is an intolerable one. The Constitution ratified in the eighteenth century formed a government "of the people, by the people, for the people." Thomas Jefferson, an Anti-Federalist, saw government as a threat to individual freedom. At this time, it was difficult for individuals and the new states to give up any of their hard-earned individual freedom to any government.

The Tenth Amendment, ratified in 1791, assured the states of their rights. The amendment reads, "The powers not delegated to the United States by the Constitution, nor prohibited by it to the states, are reserved to the states respectively, or to the people." This amendment was an attempt to ensure states of their rights and the freedom of the citizens.

The first political party in the United States was the Federalist Party. The Federalist Party was formed by Alexander Hamilton, then the Secretary of the Treasury, in 1787. The Federalist Party favored a strong central government—with all major powers existing with the central government.

Thomas Jefferson and James Madison formed an opposition party in 1791. The party was named the Democratic-Republican

Party. This party sought to limit the central government and leave control at the local or state level.

Many of the members of the first Constitutional Convention questioned the development of political parties. James Madison and other members of the Democratic-Republican Party did not trust political parties. They wanted to ban the existence of political parties. They realized citizens give up their individual freedom by joining a political party. Their hard-earned freedoms were precious. When voters support a candidate, they are exercising their freedom.

TYRANNY

Ardent political party members will not agree with this section of the book. When voters support a candidate, they are exercising their sovereignty. When voters support a party, they are delegating their sovereignty to a party. The officeholder elected by a party cannot act as an individual and support his or her own ideas—or, in many cases, the ideas of the majority of the population. They must support the party platform. Thus, political parties take away an individual voter's freedom and the freedom of the elected candidate.

As with all organizations, the leaders control the organization. When the leaders are motivated by power, the good of the party is moved aside and growth of the power of the leaders becomes the goal. While the larger number of people in a political party control more votes, many of their actions are taken to remove the individual freedom of other voters.

The leaders of a political party are power-motivated individuals. The action of a party to set the boundaries of a House district so that their party candidates can win an election is not only gerrymandering, but autocratic. This practice, like many other practices of political parties, robs some citizens of their individual freedom. One man, one vote no longer determines the victory of the candidate. A democratic republic should not operate as an autocratic society.

The Electoral College has engaged in autocratic behavior. When a state causes the vote of the Electoral College to reflect the winner of the election in the state, the voters in the state who voted for another candidate are denied their freedom. The vote of the Electoral College should reflect the percentage of the vote for each candidate in the state. There have been two instances when the Electoral College elected a president that did not receive the majority of the national vote. Thus, the leading party in the state controlled the national Electoral College election.

The Constitution recognizes the individual sovereignty of the citizen voters. All attempts by parties and individuals to subvert the power of the people should be considered a crime against the Constitution. Treason is defined as the crime of betraying one's country, especially by attempting to kill or overthrow the sovereign or government. Thus, attempts to subvert the wishes of the voters could be considered treason by the parties and individuals involved.

The author is an independent voter and does not belong to a political party.

EARLY FOREIGN AFFAIRS

There were also differences in concerns for foreign affairs between the first two political parties. The Federalists favored close relations with England, while the Democratic-Republicans favored close relations with France. France and Britain were at war at this time. The Democratic-Republicans sided with the French citizens in the French Revolution, and strongly supported individual freedom.

Naturally, European affairs played a major role in the politics of the United States. France and Britain were fighting for power. The Jay Treaty was debated by the Federalist and the states' rights groups. Thomas Jefferson hated the Jay Treaty. The XYZ affair and French thinking was interfering with trade with Britain, while the British Navy interfered with French trade. These nations were the chief trading parties of the new nation.

The interactions between the leaders of the country—especially in Congress—during this period is interesting. Those interested in the history of the nation would do well to read about the XYZ Affair. This period in history was the beginning of the United States of America's foreign policy.

The early period of the 19th century is an excellent example of the problems between government and society. The period demonstrates how decisions are made for the sake of the time. Decisions are time dependent. While individual freedom was a major concern, power motivation delayed freedom for all. The decision makers of the period were generally English (by birth) white males. They were well aware of the problems that brought them to America, and most were students of the teachings of the Age of Enlightenment.

This period continued the process of nation building that began in the previous century. The major individuals involved in the First and Second Congress and the efforts that were necessary to bring about sovereignty to the colonies were the leaders of the nation in the early nineteenth century.

Thomas Jefferson believed that the election in 1800 was as much of a revolution in the principles of our government as that of 1776. The election saved the United States from policies that endangered self-governance and threatened the groundwork of a sound republican regime.

The Constitution established a republic form of government for federal and state governments. Article 4 Section 4 also assured the states of protection in case of attack. A republican government is defined in two ways: 1) a government having a chief of state who is not a monarch and is usually a president; also a nation or other political unit having such a government. 2) a government in which supreme power is held by the citizens entitled to vote and is exercised by elected officers and representatives governing according to law; also a nation or other political unit having such a form of government.

Special attention should be given to the part of the definition that states, "A government in which supreme power is held by the citizens entitled to vote." A republic government does not give power to a political party, but supreme power to the voters. Every voter should fight all attempts to control elections.

Thomas Jefferson said, "Every generation deserves its own revolution." It may take a revolution by each generation to maintain individual freedom from excessive government rule and tyranny by the individuals in power.

The colonists had fought hard under very difficult conditions to defeat the British and to earn their sovereignty. Self-rule was on the mind of every citizen. The Articles of Confederation did not last long because the tax base favored the smaller states. This is one of the first places in our history when a tax base played a role in establishing government.

The Constitution was born with states' rights as a major point of interest. But, many members of the Congress and of the administration were Federalist in their philosophy.

The Federalist Party was formed during the Washington administration and lasted a very short time. The members of the party appear to have been more interested in personal power than in individual freedom.

The Federalist Party movement began in 1787 and lasted until 1816. Secretary of the Treasury Alexander Hamilton gathered support from the larger cities. The supporters were mostly bankers and businessmen.

Opponents of the Federalist Party were led by Thomas Jefferson and James Madison. They thought that the Federalist followers were trying to become tightly allied with the British monarchy at the expense of republican values. While the Federalist Party was supported by Northern states and the citizens of the larger cities, the supporters of individual freedom were from the agricultural states and the frontier. The supporters of sovereignty lived more independently than the citizens of the larger cities.

It was generally believed that the states could exist without the federal government, but the federal government could not exist without the consent and the support of the states. This was an observation of Joseph Store in 1833. The federal government's need of the support of the states shaped most of the decisions during these formative years.

At the beginning of the nineteenth century, the United States had grown to seventeen states. Statehood had been granted to Kentucky, Vermont, Tennessee, and Ohio. Three of the new states had two members in the House of Representatives and all four had two senators. Ohio's seats in the House of Representatives were unfilled. The Kentucky and Tennessee members were Democratic-Republicans, while Vermont had one Democratic Republican member and one member of the Federalist Party.

In government, the power motive is always a problem for the governed. Power motivates individuals to promote themselves and makes them less concerned with affairs of the nation and the welfare of others. Organizations are formed by academic thinkers with objectives of good for the welfare of others.

When the power-motivated individuals seek and gain power, the objectives of the organization give way to symbols of power. The more individuals, groups, and departments an individual motivated by power can have reporting to himself or herself, the greater his or her power Power motivation is a major cause of excessive overhead spending.

Giving up power for individual freedom has always been difficult to accomplish. As the Constitution was being written, the new states were writing their own constitutions. Voting rights were restricted to landowners. State legislatures retained the right to elect senators to the federal Congress until 1913. It is obvious that power motivation is always at work in governments. The male ego was also at work, but gender is not mentioned. Women remained at home during the eighteenth century and were not part of the government or the workforce.

The interest in sovereignty and self-rule continued after the ratification of the Constitution of the United States. In fact, it took several years before all the states ratified the Constitution. Segregationists—active mainly in the Southern states and one or two Northern states—grew stronger because of the slavery issue. While South Carolina was one of the first states to join the Union in 1788, it attempted to leave the Union as early as 1832. Alabama joined the Union in 1813.

Jacksonian Democracy between 1820 and 1830 lessened

the fear that individual freedom would destroy the nation. Federalists were power motivated and fought for central control. Democracy was on the rise and federalism suffered loss of control in Congress. While Jackson was president, he had to send troops to South Carolina to prevent secession in 1832.

In 1838, the United States went to war with Mexico. The war lasted two years. The class of 1846 from West Point played a major part in the war. These same class brothers became generals on both sides of the Civil War. Tom "Stonewall" Jackson struggled at West Point, but distinguished himself in the Mexican War. He was a Southern general. George McClellan, a distinguished student, became a Northern general. The treaty following the Mexican War greatly increased the number of square miles of United States territory. The expansion into the new territories brought on the Indian wars.

During the first half of the nineteenth century, both states' rights and individual freedom played a great role in the history of the United States of America.

While there were slave owners in the Northern states, many of the industrial states, mainly in the North, were against slavery. New York and New Jersey were early in their calls for freeing slaves. New York promised freedom to the slaves who helped fight the British. They believed in the freedom of mankind.

There where riots over slavery in New York. Individuals, especially Irish immigrants, fought over jobs. The Southern agricultural states were very interested in their own sovereignty— and were in favor of slavery. This period was the era of the great debates in society and in the Congress.

When one reads the 1860 "Declaration of the Immediate Causes Which Induce and Justify the Secession of South

Carolina from the Federal Union" and the declarations of other states, including Georgia, Mississippi, and Texas, it is obvious that these states considered the federal Congress intolerable.

They believed strongly that the states had the right to dissolve the Union. They declared that non-slave states were not living up to state sovereignty granted to the states by the Tenth Amendment to the Constitution.

The slave states believed in state sovereignty and not federal control. They believed that Congress wanted to make laws that affected the states and that the Constitution did not grant the Congress that power. Another war was fought between those in favor of individual sovereignty and those motivated by power.

While the Southern agricultural states claimed individual sovereignty, it was not granted to the slaves. In 1863, the Emancipation Proclamation ended slavery. It was another hundred years before the Civil Rights Acts were passed. Once again, power-motivated individuals believed in individual sovereignty for themselves, but denied freedom to others. While race was a concern, gender remained absent from all discussions of individual sovereignty.

In the early twentieth century, women won the right to hold office. Women entered the workforce in larger numbers during this same period. They work mainly in offices, nursing, and similar jobs. As education became more available to women, they took jobs in the professions, especially teaching. They were not members of the male labor force. It was not until the late twentieth century that the United Nations recognized women's rights.

In order to control voting by race, the Southern states passed a poll tax law after the Civil War. While everyone was required to pay the tax before they voted, this tax greatly disadvantaged individuals with a minimum income. Women could not vote. Once again, power motivation won out over individual freedom.

While women's rights actions predate the Civil War, little was accomplished for a long time. In 1848, sixty-eight women and thirty-two men met in New York. Their Declaration of Sentiments stated women's grievances and started the women's rights movement.

Little progress was made for the next twenty years. In 1869, Susan Anthony and Elizabeth Stanton organized the National Woman Suffrage Association. In this same year, Lucy Stone and Henry Blackwell decided a better attack for woman suffrage would be to work through the states. In December, Wyoming granted woman suffrage. In 1893, more states granted women the right to vote. It is interesting that the gender change began almost thirty years after the race change. Slaves were granted full citizenship in the 1860s. It was not until 1920 that the Nineteenth Amendment granted women suffrage.

The Age of Enlightenment began in the early 1700s and the Civil Rights Acts were passed in the 1960s. Individual freedom has been a long, slow process in the United States. Today, history textbooks pay little attention to individual freedom and the long struggle.

The philosophy that began in the early days of the Age of Enlightenment are the source behind the struggles for freedom today. In the West, individuals demand their rights, while the Middle East is controlled by male-dominated religious societies governed by autocrats.

The struggles in the Middle East are a continuation of the much earlier struggles in the West. The framers of the Constitution were intelligent enough to recognize the problems caused by the mixture of religion and government in Europe. Thomas Paine recognized that mixing social functions and government functions always causes problems. Society and government have had trouble existing together in the Middle East for thousands of years. After almost 250 years, the United States still has problems caused by mixing social function and government functions.

While Jackson's democracy advocated one man, one vote, the attainment of the idea is not even met today. The Articles of Confederation gave the states equal rights in Congress. Large states were funding the government and wanted more power in government. The Constitution set up a House of Representatives that gave equal populations a member. The bicameral Congress and the growth of the population have eliminated the one man one vote concept.

The small states each have two senators. It takes ten states to equal the population of California. Thus ten small states control 20 percent of the Senate vote and California controls 2 percent. The four large states control 35 percent of the members of the House, while twelve of the smaller states only control three-hundreds of a percent. The twelve small states have twenty-four senators.

Since at least three smaller states have populations less than the average number of 650,000 required for a House seat, they each have three members of Congress. Each state has two senators. The two senators from small states represent a small number of citizens, while the two senators from California represent over 36,000,000 citizens and the two senators from Texas represent over 25,000,000 citizens. The two senators from the other two large states, Florida and New York, represent about 20,000,000. Each member of the House of

Representatives represents about the same number of citizens. With this type of representation we no longer have a one man one vote system.

When one examines the organization of the new federal government, it appears that the Federalists were correct. Having a strong, organized federal government was less expensive than each of the thirteen states forming strong governments. But this decision did not take into account the citizen interest in freedom and self-rule. The decision also didn't consider the growth and diversity of today's nation.

CHAPTER 4
NECESSARY CHANGES IN GOVERNMENT

While in the eighteenth century a strong federal government was desired to support development and a great international image, the large area and population of the United States today requires greater local area sovereignty. Like the actions of the British Empire taken to promote sovereignty in the various parts of the empire held it together, all areas of the nation need greater sovereignty. Granting greater freedoms for self-rule will support national growth. The reduction in the federal government will greatly reduce the cost of administration. With greater freedom in various parts of the nation, laws can be enacted that support local development. Proper organization of the areas will produce a sufficient tax base to support the government. In the eighteenth century the nation gained from having a strong Federal government. In the twenty-first century the nation is the sum of its parts. The stronger each part becomes the stronger the nation will be.

The United States budget has concerned the individuals

in power since the framing of the first Constitution. Where is Thomas Jefferson when you need him?

In 1798, Jefferson wanted the federal budget maintained without the power to borrow money. Jefferson wrote, "I wish it were possible to obtain a single amendment to our Constitution. I would be willing to depend on that alone for the reduction of the administration of our government." Jefferson appeared concerned that control of government by power-motivated individuals would excessively increase the size and the administrative cost of governments.

Jefferson believed that a balanced budget would maintain the genuine principles of the Constitution. He wanted an article that would take away the federal government's power to borrow.

Without the power to borrow money, all governments would require a surplus fund. Income and expenses are difficult to balance. Maintaining a surplus fund limits this problem. Another way to limit the budgeting problem is to control administrative overhead. As Jefferson said, governments would limit their overhead cost if they could not borrow money. Today we have excessive debt and excessive government administrative costs.

The recent recession and the magnitude of the decrease in individual and government wealth are causing problems with financing governments. It appears that the actions taken by Congress and the president, especially with the stimulus package, have contributed to greater debt at the state level.

The overspending during the good times and the loss of wealth in the recession has the states in financial difficulty. They must reduce their budgets. While they are reducing the pay of government employees, there is not a reduction in the number and size of government bodies, such as the legislature. Do we need a bicameral state legislature?

The Constitution grants the power to control spending to the House of Representatives. All money bills must begin in the House. The size of the House has increased from one member for every 30,000 citizens to one member for approximately 650,000 citizens. Thus there are 435 House members.

The nation has grown from just over a million citizens to over three hundred million citizens. Citizens knew their House member when they represented thirty thousand citizens. Today, many citizens do not know the name of their House member; certainly they do not know the representative personally. In the voting booth, they pull the handle that votes for the candidates of a party.

It is time for a constitutional convention. Government can be different from the status quo; it can be effective and efficient when it is properly organized. There are many ways to organize government so that it provides effective, efficient government. The members of the convention need to be imaginative. There must be thinking outside the box.

It would be much easier to form an effective and efficient government at all levels of government if this was the eighteenth century. As Thomas Paine stated, society in every state is a blessing. Our neighborhoods, cities, counties, and states are known to everyone. Our society is a blessing. But social and government organization are formed for different reasons. Governments are formed to provide services that are paid for by the taxpayers.

There are two major concerns that the Constitutional Convention must address: Reducing government overhead and establishing a tax base for each government sufficient to support the budget. The new Constitution should require a yearly balanced budget by all the governments—and the budget should include a sufficient surplus fund.

Since the economy and the tax income vary, a surplus fund is needed to cover short-term differences in income and expenses. When the surplus fund is used, it should be refunded as soon as possible. The possible period should be no more than four years.

Study of the development of federal, state, county, and local governments shows a complete disregard for factors that have an effect on their efficiency and effectiveness. The excessive number of governments and the lack of proper organization of the governments results in a rip-off of taxpayers. Excessive numbers of governments require excessive administrative cost. Since no government position is an entitlement granted by the Constitution, they are subject to change.

The constitution sets a procedure for changes in state borders. This requires approve of the state legislature and the congress.

In the eighteenth century, about half the population in the agricultural Southern states were slaves. At the time statehood was granted, there was no consideration of population or area governed. As a result of this disorganized growth, borders have developed without consideration of a tax base sufficient to support the budget and the excessive governments, but each has overhead cost for administration.

The various states have major differences. The natural resources vary greatly from state to state. Some states have large agricultural income; other states rely on industry for income; while other states have a mixture of agriculture and industrial for income. Coastal states derive income from trade.

If a Constitutional Congress properly organized federal, state, and local governments, there would be a savings of billions of dollars. These savings are not a one-time savings, but will continue each year. These dollars are currently being ripped off from taxpayers to support excessive government overhead. The billions in savings could be used to pay off the trillions of dollars of current debt. Paying off debt saves money paid in interest on the debt.

What does federal government administration cost? The first Congress and each Congress until 1815 received just six dollars a day while the Congress was in session. By 2006, congresspersons received a yearly salary of $165,200. The leaders receive larger salaries. These salaries range from $212,100 to around $183,000.

Their other privileges include an office and a staff. The staff pay ranges around $160,000 per year. These salaries are compared to the average yearly income of $45,000 for men and $35,000 for women.

The costs listed in the above paragraph apply only to the federal Congress. The state legislatures and the county and city councils receive about the same pay as a congressperson. Think of the cost of over 18,000 state, county, and local governments that taxpayers support today. The state legislatures are generally larger than county councils and local councils. When these legislatures and councils are composed of only ten members, the administrative cost to the taxpayer is $1.6 million per year. There are additional costs for office and other expenses—and the perks the administrators have granted to themselves.

While the Constitution established the status quo bicameral Congress, the Constitution does not give entitlement to the positions in the House of Representatives or the Senate. There are great concerns in Congress about the entitlements of citizens written into laws, but there is no discussion about the lawmakers' entitlement to their positions.

CHAPTER 5
ORGANIZING GOVERNMENTS

Does the nation really need 18,000 governments to supply the service need by the citizens? Or, could the governments be better organized to assure "safety and happiness."

While reducing the number of county and local governments is important, the actions required to reduce these governments is easy as compared to the action necessary to change the federal and state governments.

There are many instances where cities have moved their borders to increase their size and tax base. There are several instances where the city and the county borders have become the same. These actions reduce cost and increase the tax base.

As stated by Thomas Paine, society must be a major consideration in organizing a new government. The citizens have grown used to their environment. Reorganization should be for government reasons. Existing borders for states, counties, and local governments may be retained for social reasons. But establishing new government areas will be necessary in order to establish efficiency and effectiveness in the government

Currently, local governments have a two-tiers approach to government. There are governments that are normally called counties. Some states have other names such as parishes in Louisiana or boroughs in Alaska. In most states, the counties are divided into municipalities. The governmental structures of municipalities are generally controlled by the state's Constitution.

While the federal government and the state governments are bicameral governments, the county and municipalities are generally one chamber governments. They are called councils, either county councils or city councils. Depending on the population and the area governed, the councils are assisted by boards, committees, and other named groups that provide government services to districts. All of the government functions cost taxpayers overhead.

There are substantial differences in the population and area served by county and municipal governments. Municipalities like New York City, Chicago, and Los Angles have populations in the millions, while Jenkins, Minnesota has a population of 287. Fortunately, the very small local governments are served by citizen volunteers.

In the fifty states, there are 3,033 counties. If on the average there were only five paid municipality governments for the 3,033, there would be 15,165 municipality governments. Therefore, the estimated number of local governments in the two-tiered system is 18,248.

With the conservative estimate of municipality governments and a population of just over three hundred million, on the average 16,867 citizens are paying for a municipal government, a county government, a state government, and a federal government.

It is obvious that on the average approximately seventeen thousand citizens are paying the administrative overhead cost of four governments. This is an excessive taxpayer cost. Merger of governments reduces administrative cost. The Mergers of municipal governments with county governments is a good example. County governments can be merged to reduce cost. Especially, counties with small populations should be merged to reduce administrative cost.

The lucky citizens are the ones who do not live in a municipal government, but live in the county. They get the services they need and do not pay the extra administrative overhead.

CHAPTER 6

REDUCE GOVERNMENT AND SAVE TAX DOLLARS

The size and the population of the fifty states show great variations. The number of counties per state also varies. Georgia has a population near ten million and has 159 counties, while California with a population of above thirty-six million has just fifty-eight counties. Certainly tax base was not a consideration when the counties were formed.

Taxpayers in states with excessive numbers of counties are paying more taxes to cover the cost of administration in their budget or the county is in debt—more likely other taxpayers are subsidizing the counties.

There is an urgent need for merger of state governments. However, the present Constitution forbids changes in state borders without the consent of the state's legislature and the federal legislature. Citizens have become attached to their state borders. For major changes in the federal government, a constitutional convention will be required to organize all governments and their various functions.

There is no reason for the complete lack of organization in the county governments in the present states. Taxpayer and voter actions can bring about needed mergers. This lack of organization is costing taxpayers billions of dollars. These dollars are needed to balance budgets. The current spending on borrowed money must come to an end.

The following data was included in *Save Tax Dollars*. It is important to compare the populations of the states and the number of counties within a state. The lack of thought about organization over the years is obvious from the data presented.

Alabama: The population of Alabama is 4,500,752. There are sixty-seven counties in the state. The median population of the sixty-seven counties is 67,185. This is about the population of a small city. The state has a general funds budget of $1.5 billion dollars, and is expecting a major shortfall in 2010.

Alaska: This state is different from all the other states. Alaska has a population of 648,818. But they still have 16 boroughs. Thus, the median population for each borough is 40,551. In addition to the 16 boroughs, Alaska has many smaller area governments called counties. Alaska has money from the sale of oil, but they are wasting money on local government.

Arkansas: The population of Arkansas is 2,855,390. The state has seventy-five counties. The median population of the 75 counties is only 38,886 people. Many of the counties in

Arkansas have less than ten thousand people. The smallest, Calhoun County, has only 5,435 people.

Arizona: The population of Arizona is 6,500,180. Almost half the population resides in Maricopa County, which has a population of 3,072,149. The state has fifteen counties. Therefore, 3,428,031 people reside in the remaining fourteen counties. If 3,072,149 people can be governed by one county government, why does it take fourteen counties to govern 3,428,031 people?

California: The population of California is 36,756,666. This is the largest population of all the states in the Union. With this large population, California has fifty-eight counties. This is eighteen counties less than Arkansas. With just five states considered so far, we see that the current organization of the fifty states is very random—and very little thought has gone into state and county organization.

Colorado: The population of Colorado is 4,939,456. The state has sixty-four counties. Thus, the median population for the sixty-four counties is 77,804. The population of two counties, Denver and Arapahoe, make up more than a million people of the almost five million people in the state. Baca County has only 3,834 people and appears to be losing population. Broomfield County was added in 1998. Instead of a merger, it appears that Colorado is increasing administrative overhead.

Connecticut: The current population of Connecticut is 3,518,285. There are eight counties in the state. Arizona requires fourteen counties to govern this many people.

Delaware: This is another small state with a population of 885,969. Yet, Delaware has two senators—the same number as Texas and New York. Naturally, with only three counties, the number of representatives is very few. This is a great place for merger. Maryland and Delaware should consider a merger. This would reduce the number of senators by two and increase the number of representatives for Maryland.

Florida: The population of Florida is 18,537,969. There are sixty-seven counties in the state. With half the population of California, Florida has more county governments. Until the recent recession, Florida was one of the fastest growing states in the Union. Florida should consider a merger of counties and a discontinuation of local governments. These mergers would provide much needed capital for services and projects in the state. The state officials, including the governor, are complaining about state budget problems. But, they ignore the benefit of a merger to reduce overhead cost.

Georgia: This state is an excellent example of too many county governments. While the population of the state is 9,829,211, there are 159 counties. Several counties have less than two or three thousand people. While Fulton County has 1,033,756, Glascock has only 2,801 people. If one county is operating with a population of one million, why not have all counties have at least one million people and reduce the number of local governments? The taxpayers should appreciate the savings by these mergers.

Hawaii: Hawaii and Alaska are different from the other forty-eight states. Hawaii has a population of 1,295,178 and has four counties. These counties are on the various islands. Alaska has a population of only 648,818 and has sixteen boroughs. Hawaii operates with just one board of education. Think of the dollars we would have for student education if each state had one superintendent of education and one board of education. Small offices located around the state could handle contracts and other business affairs.

Idaho: The population of Idaho is 1,545,801 with forty-four county governments. What do you think of this state and local government organization?

Illinois: This is a very interesting state in terms of lack of thought and organization of its government. The state population is 12,910,409. Cook County has a population of 5,256,037. There are 102 counties. Pope County has just 3,991 people, and Stark County has 6,019. With the government of Chicago and Cook County as an example, it seems that taxpayers should have realized that they were paying too much for county and local government. With this example of Cook County and Chicago there for all to see, it seems action would be taken to better organize the government. Maybe they never heard of a merger.

Indiana: The population of Indiana is 6,423,113, with ninety-two counties. Once again, the borders of Randolph County were changed to form a few new counties in 1998. Spending tax funds on government overhead could not have been a factor in this government decision.

Iowa: The population of Iowa is 3,067,856, with ninety-seven counties. With only half the population of Indiana, Iowa has more county governments.

Kansas: The population of Kansas is 2,818,747, with 105 counties. Three states—Indiana, Iowa, and Kansas—are good examples of the lack of planning that has gone into state and county government. We are now in the twenty-first century, and the United States was established in the late eighteenth century. Over these years, one would think either the federal government or state governments would have realized governments need thoughtful organization. We have state governors who meet regularly. What do they work on at these meetings? It is time taxpayers regularly asked, "What do they work on at these meetings?"

Kentucky: The population of Kentucky is 4,314,113. The state has 120 counties. This is the third-largest number of county governments among the fifty states. Kentucky recognized that many of its counties did not have a sufficient tax base to support the needed services, but the people voted to keep their county borders. Is it any wonder why the mountain areas have a high poverty level?

Louisiana: The population of Louisiana is 4,492,076. There are sixty counties in the state. Kentucky has about the same population as Louisiana, but Kentucky has twice the number of counties. The Kentucky state budget is $456 million, while the Louisiana state budget is $341 million. This is a difference of $115 million. While the federal government deals in billions and trillions of dollars, $115 million would reduce the debt of many states.

Maine: The population of Maine is 1,318,301 and the state has sixteen counties.

Maryland: The population of Maryland is 5,699,478 and the state has twenty-three counties.

Massachusetts: The population of Massachusetts is 6,593,587. There are six counties in the state. The size of the state in area seems to be more of a factor in deciding the number of counties than the support of taxpayer dollars.

Michigan: The population of Michigan is 9,969,727, and there are eighty-three counties. Michigan is one of the states hardest hit by the 2008 recession, with a large gap between income and expenses.

Minnesota: The population of Minnesota is 5,266,214 and the number of counties is eighty-seven.

Mississippi: The population of Mississippi is 2,951,996 with eighty-two county governments. The budgets of Minnesota and Mississippi differ by only $19 million. Mississippi ranks last in the fifty states in many areas. Saving tax dollars by merger considerations could help the budget.

Missouri: The population of Missouri is 5,987,580 and there are 114 counties in the state. While the populations of Minnesota and Missouri are not very different, the state budgets differ by $353 million. That is twice the last comparison of the difference in the budgets of two states.

Montana: Montana is one of the states with a population of less than one million. The population of the state is 935,670 and there are fifty-four county governments. North and South Dakota each have a population of less than one million. These small states contribute two senators each. While this representation is supposed to be offset by number of representatives, the Senate remains a very important governing body. This is an area of the country where mergers should be considered.

Nebraska: The population of Nebraska is 1,756,787 and there are ninety-three counties. While pride in state and county governments must be considered, it pales in comparison to the savings in tax dollars that could be obtained with consideration of government efficiency. Mergers of states in this area of the country would reduce cost of government for the state taxpayers and reduce the cost of federal government by reducing the number of senators.

Nevada: The population of this state is 2,414,807, and there are sixteen counties.

New Hampshire: The population of New Hampshire is 1,309,946, and the state has ten counties.

New Jersey: New Jersey's population is 8,717,925 and there are twenty-one counties. With New York City and New York State as examples, one would think that New Jersey would realize that their governments are not operating efficiently.

New Mexico: The population is 1,928,384 and there are thirty-three counties in New Mexico. When New Mexico and Arizona were admitted to the Union, tax base was not a consideration.

Merger of these two states would reduce overhead and improve tax base.

New York: The population of New York is 19,254,630 and there are fifty-seven counties. New York City has a population similar to the population of New Jersey. The population of New York City is 8,214,426. New York State could benefit from merger of county and local governments.

North Carolina: The population of North Carolina is 8,683,242 and the state has one hundred counties—twice the number of counties in New York. While New Jersey operates with an excessive number of counties at twenty-one, North Carolina has one hundred. The populations of New Jersey and North Carolina are about the same size as New York City.

North Dakota: This is one of the smallest population numbers of all the states at 636,673. The average population of a US representative district is 650,000. The number of counties in the state is fifty-three.

Ohio: The population is 11,464,042 and there are eighty-eight counties.

Oklahoma: The population of Oklahoma is 3,547,884, with seventy-seven counties.

Oregon: Oregon has a population of 3,641,056, with thirty-six counties. While the population of Oklahoma and Oregon are nearly the same, Oklahoma has twice as many county governments that require funding from the tax dollars.

Pennsylvania: The population is 12,429,616 and there are sixty-six county governments.

Rhode Island: Rhode Island is one of the smallest states in area and has a small population for an Eastern state. The population is 1,076,189 and there are six counties. Does this suggest to you that merger should be considered?

South Carolina: South Carolina is a small state in terms of area, but like most of the original thirteen colonies, the population is larger. The population of South Carolina is 4,255,083 and there are forty-six county governments. South Carolina has just eleven counties less than New York does. The author hopes that by now you can see the need for merger.

South Dakota: Both South Dakota and North Dakota have very small populations. The population of South Dakota is 775,933 and there are sixty-four county governments. Thus, with just more than one million people, North and South Dakota require 117 county governments. This is an excellent example of where merger would reduce overhead.

Tennessee: Tennessee has a population of 5,962,956, and there are ninety-three counties.

Texas: Texas and California are both large in area and have large populations. The population of Texas is 22,859,968 and there are 254 counties. Harris County has the largest population. There are 3,984,349 people in the county, with 2,144,491 people living in Houston.

Utah: The population of Utah is 2,469,585 and there are twenty-nine counties.

Vermont: The population of this state is 623,050 and there are fourteen counties. When you compare Vermont with North and South Dakota, one can see the need for merger of county governments. While merger of state governments would be a larger problem, these data support the suggested merger of state governments.

Virginia: Virginia was the largest of the original thirteen states, and its population is 7,567,465—and there are ninety-five county governments in the state.

Washington: The population of Washington is 6,287,759 and there are thirty-nine counties.

West Virginia: The population of West Virginia is 1,816,856 and there are fifty-five county governments.

Wisconsin: The population of this state is 5,536,201 and there are seventy-two counties.

Wyoming: The population of Wyoming is lower than the population of either North or South Dakota. The population of Wyoming is 509,294 and there are twenty-three county governments in the state. While the average population required for a representative in Congress is 650,000, Wyoming has one representative and, of course, two senators. Is this really one person, one vote?

The above data support the need for states to merge their

county governments. The lack of planning in the Constitution and by Congress for states joining the Union is very obvious. It will be extremely difficult to correct this error without a constitutional convention.

While the stated populations may be in error, any errors are small enough to be insufficient to change the conclusions. Counting populations is not an exact science. Some areas of the country are growing at a very rapid rate and some areas are losing population.

Nebraska is an interesting state to review; the data regarding the lack of consideration of economic factors in the state, county, and local government's organization is obvious.

Nebraska is the one state that does not have a bicameral legislature. There is just one legislative body, the Senate. The citizens should be complimented for this thoughtfulness. There are forty-nine senators and the state population is 1,769,619. That is one senator for every 36,665 citizens. This represents about one state senator for half the number of citizens in a federal house district.

While Nebraska saves tax dollars with their one-chamber state legislature, there are an excessive number of senators. If the senate was approximately half its size, they would save more tax dollars.

There are ninety-three counties with an average population of about two thousand. Almost half the state population lives in Omaha or Lincoln. So many counties are unnecessary—especially since half the population lives in two cities. Merger of county governments would reduce administrative cost and save tax dollars.

Nebraska should be complimented for being the one state that realized that a House of Representatives was an unnecessary expense for a state. In fact, the federal House of Representatives in Congress is an unnecessary expense in the twenty-first century. With Senate districts of near equal populations electing a senator, there would be a return to the one man, one vote concept. At present, there is no need for two senators from each state. The state populations vary from less than one million to over thirty-six million.

Nebraska has an excellent Internet website that describes its government. The site can be found online at http://nebraskalegislature/pdf/bluebook/805-888.pdf. The legislature has passed laws that classify incorporated municipalities. There are five categories for municipalities that are based upon their population. Metropolitan Class Cities have populations of three hundred thousand or more citizens. Primary Class Cities have populations between 295,999 and 100,001 citizens. First Class Cities have populations between 100,000 and 5,001 citizens. Second Class Cities have populations between 5,001 and 801 citizens. Finally, Villages have populations between 800 and 100 citizens.

According to their website, there are 383 villages, 115 second class cites, 30 first class cities, and one metropolitan city. There are 529 local governments, 93 county governments, in addition to the state government. The population of Nebraska is 1,756,787 citizens.

In addition to the governments listed, Nebraska has an Association of County Officials that is a nonprofit organization. There is also a League of Municipalities with a fifteen-member board.

If Nebraska reduced its number of senators, merged counties, and required municipalities below the Primary Class to merge with county governments or have volunteers for their city councils, they would reduce administrative costs.

With this example, little else needs to be said about excessive government. Minnesota—a state with a population over five million—has eighteen cities with populations of fifty thousand or more.

All states should have a legislature with just one chamber. The state senators are elected from a district. Therefore, the senators represent the one man, one vote concept. Unlike the federal government where the senators represent a state and the House of Representatives was formed to give states with different populations better representation, the state senators represent nearly equal populations. The number of state senate districts should be carefully controlled to reduce administrative costs.

CHAPTER 7
ONE SIZE DOES NOT FIT ALL

The 535 lawmakers in Washington are a tremendous and unnecessary expense. The 435-member House, salaries for representatives, large office expenses, unneeded perks, and the pork added to bills is excessive spending.

The original size of the country and its small population supported a strong federal government in the eighteenth century. Today, the country has 3.5 million square miles and a population of 308 million. It is time for reduction in the size of the federal government and increased sovereignty for the various areas of the country.

Energy is required to support development and production. Some areas of the country have hydroelectric power, wind power, or solar power. The agricultural areas can develop biofuels. Decisions on energy would be better if they were made by local areas rather than an Energy Department in Washington. Do you know of any accomplishment by the Department of Energy since its inception? The author does not know of any accomplishments.

Another example of the need to move Washington functions to local functions is the Department of Housing and Urban Development. All development is not urban. Agricultural areas need development controls for subdivisions and farms. When development is controlled locally, decisions are made closer to the affected people—and all the factors involved in the decision are known to those making the decisions.

With careful study and a collective search for wisdom, all governments could be improved. Over time, changes affect the function and the efficiency of governments and their organization. One function of all governments that is necessary is a committee to review and evaluate the government and its functions. When changes are made in a timely manner, the changes are easier to make and less disruptive. All the present governments have not followed this type of action—and the resulting dysfunction and inefficiency is obvious.

Over the last two hundred years, we have seen excessive growth of the federal government. This is especially true in the last fifty years—and there will be a greater rate of growth in the future. Population increases at an exponential rate. Larger populations have greater growth rates.

The larger the population becomes, the greater the number of problems. When there is a government problem, the method used to solve the problem is the creation of another layer of government. Each layer adds administrative spending to the budget. Frequently, the suggested method for solving the problem is the elimination of government programs that help the people. The elimination of the programs hurts the citizens— while the new layer of government adds to the dysfunction and the cost.

The president's Commission on the Budget was entirely

composed of old government employees—the same people who allowed the excessive overgrowth of the dysfunctional, inefficient government of today. While these individuals had lived off the government for their working years and were living on government retirement, they complained about the problems of supporting senior citizens.

When corporations have financial problems, they look for reductions in administrative costs. Middle management is usually the first area reduced in size. Mergers are used by corporations to increase market share and reduce administrative spending. Market share must support the company and provide a profit. Taxpayers are like market share in that they support the government.

Another concept used by corporations deals with increasing corporate size. When management by a chief executive officer and a corporate board becomes excessive, the corporation is divided into profit centers. This brings decision making nearer to the areas affected by the decision. The size of the area of the country and the population has increased the complications for the federal government. The government is excessive and the budget is so large that the GAO cannot keep track of the expenses. It is time that many of the federal functions were transferred to different areas of the country.

The excessive number of congressmen and the size of the executive branch have caused the government to become dysfunctional. There are too many areas of overlapping responsibility. The system with two parties has added to this dysfunction. Today, when politicians engage in debates, the debates are composed of individual fiat and the country has lost the leadership that could be provided by a collective search for wisdom. The members of the legislature use the hearings and debates for their reelection and not for the good of the country.

The Constitution includes a method for amendment of the document. But after more than two hundred years, it is time for the formation of effective and efficient governments to ensure, as stated in the Declaration of Independence, the "safety and happiness" of the citizens. Study of every executive department is needed. Some should be eliminated and others transferred to state function.

At the state level, either the taxpayers in states with excessive numbers of counties are paying more taxes to cover the cost of administration in their budget, or the county is in debt. Most likely, other taxpayers are subsidizing other counties.

Thomas Jefferson wanted a Constitutional amendment that prevented government from borrowing money. He said, "The reorganized governments should be prevented from borrowing." Jefferson thought, and it is obvious, that if governments could not borrow, they would have to control all spending, including administrative overhead.

Yet, borrowing has supported increases in overhead spending. Even with their financial troubles, states are not looking inward to control the budget. They are looking outward. They want to reduce the salaries and benefits of government workers who provide services to the citizens. The federal and state senators and representatives do not have entitlement to their offices. A careful review of each elected office and government administrative position should be made. These reductions in costs should come before reductions in services to taxpayers.

Study of the development of federal, state, county, and local governments show a complete disregard for factors that have an effect on their efficiency and effectiveness. The excessive size of government administrations and the lack of proper organization of the governments results in a rip-off of taxpayers. Excessive numbers of governments require excessive administrative costs. Since no government position is an entitlement granted by the Constitution, they are all subject to elimination.

CHAPTER 8
PROBLEMS WITH GOVERNMENT BEGAN EARLY

The leaders of the country in the 1800s were dealing with 1800s problems. The Constitution had to be approved by the states. Thus, many of the problems leaders of the country faced are the results of problem that began in the previous century.

At the time statehood was granted, there was no consideration of population or area governed. As a result of this disorganized growth, borders have developed without consideration of a tax base sufficient to support the budget, and the excessive governments each have overhead costs for administration. Remember that most taxpayers are currently supporting four governments in order to achieve the services that provide "safety and happiness."

Today, the states and citizens support the need for a federal government. But, the citizens should not forget their states' rights and the citizens should not forget their individual freedom. Too many citizens have given their lives in support of these sovereignties.

As previously mentioned, there are great differences in the

various areas of the country. Sources of energy are a major concern. While some states have hydroelectric power, others could develop more solar, wind, or biofuels. The United States has many nuclear plants.

The government and the tax structure of the states need to be different. Decision-making needs to be nearer to the individuals affected by the decisions and not in Washington.

If federal, state, and local governments were properly organized, there would be savings of billions of dollars. This reorganization includes a reduction in the number of states. A constitutional convention could make a very careful evaluation of the size and population that is required for statehood. The government divisions within a state require the same careful consideration. How much government administrative cost is necessary to provide the citizens with the services they need? It should always be remembered that governments exist for "the safety and happiness" of the citizens.

The author agrees with Thomas Paine that society is to be valued and governments are a necessary evil. The data from the Rand McNally Road *Atlas* shows that many areas with names do not have governments. It indicates that these areas are largely social areas. They have borders like areas with governments.

The areas without governments receive their government services from a surrounding area. They pay taxes for these services outside their named area. This data supports the idea that there can be social areas and government areas. When borders that exist for government reasons are moved, there is not a need for changing the social borders or their names.

The social areas can keep their names, borders, addresses, and all the services that they now receive from corporations, such as post offices and telephone companies. Their government services will be the same, but where they pay taxes will change.

CHAPTER 9
FUNDING GOVERNMENTS

Sales tax is widely used by states and local governments. Item tax is used by all branches of government. Luxury items are taxed. Food and medicine are absolutely needed items, but luxury items are not needed. Taxing property, especially real estate, has always been popular with governments. In general, when a project of service is voted into law, there is tax put in place to fund the project or service. For example, the gasoline tax is used to support road and street projects. As with all taxes, the tax burden on the citizen taxed must be carefully evaluated.

We have had a graduated income tax for about one hundred years. By definition, this process is designed to support society with less income at the expense of the society with income beyond that required to support their needs. A flat income tax has been proposed many times.

A flat rate tax takes the same percent of the income from all earners. Currently, the amount paid increases as the earned income increases. The current tax codes are very large and complicated. Attempts should be made to simplify tax codes. It should be remember that taxes should only be used to fund the government. Tax breaks complicate the tax codes.

The value added tax is used by many European countries. France is very fond of the value added tax system. France claims that this tax is easy to audit and simplifies the tax codes. A tax is assessed at each level of the production of a product. The materials used in the next level of production are taxed. The company records of their production are used to audit the tax. Unlike sales tax—where records can be changed or unreported—value added tax is more accurately collected. Naturally, the tax is added to the price of the product at the end of production. The tax is collected from the manufacturer rather than at the time of sale.

American citizens are used to taxes charged at the sale of products. Sales taxes, gasoline taxes, and luxury taxes are examples. When taxes are charged on products and services, the taxes should be dedicated to a purpose. For example, gasoline taxes should only be used for building and maintaining transportation functions.

In all cases, the tax base and the expense must be balanced. General funds and discretionary funds should not be allowed. These funds are used unnecessarily—and they promote excessive government spending.

Some congresspersons seem to have crystal balls. They sign pledges that they will not increase taxes. Time and situations change that may require tax adjustments.

CHAPTER 10

DOING THE SAME THING AND EXPECTING A DIFFERENT RESULT

Outside the box thinking brings openness and new ways of viewing problems. Thus, problem solving is not limited to the status quo. It is time that taxpayers and voters begin to think outside the box and bring about major changes in all of our governments. The aforementioned data on tax savings makes these radical changes in governments more attractive.

The oversized and dysfunctional federal government is adding to the nation's problems and the national debt. This is the result of thinking inside the box. The bickering two-major-party system has members who are more interested in promotion of the party and destruction of the other party than they are in providing for the national interest. Daily, we see individual fiat and a lack of a collective search for wisdom.

The two parties and the voters frequently elect attorneys to office. The law school and the profession teach and train attorneys to be adversaries. They argue one side of the question.

It is difficult, if not impossible, to have a collective search for wisdom in an adversarial environment.

While individual fiat does not solve problems or aid decision making, a collective search for wisdom is needed. A collective search for wisdom is not listening to a very vocal minority. It is the silent majority that must be heard.

If taxpayers are tired of inside-the-box thinking and accept outside-the-box thinking, they can come together—as Americans always have—to solve the problems through a collective search for wisdom. Working together, the taxpayers and voters can take back government from Washington and return it to Main Street.

When the nation was founded, there was a need for a strong federal government to support national development. Today, the population is very large and spread out. The federal government did nothing to prevent the recent recession. It is time that control moved to Main Street. The wide variations in the country call for local control to increase local development. The United States is no longer a small nation; today, the United States is the sum of the nation's parts.

Less government has always been the best government. But like everything else, government promotes itself. With power-motivated people in charge, growth under the individual increases the individual's power. As you look back over history, each major problem has not been solved by changes in leadership. Instead, another layer of government has been put in place. Increasing government is the power-motivated individual's method of problem solving.

Many times, the corporation is divided into new corporations. Sections and areas of the major corporation are brought together in order to provide an effective, efficient operation. The market share of the products produced is large enough to support the corporation and provide a profit. It is time that local areas were organized in an effective, efficient manner. The tax base should be sufficient to support the area's government. Borrowing money is not the answer to a financial problem; reorganization is frequently the best answer to the problem.

Government borders can exist for organization of government. This is true of city governments and county governments. Changing government borders should be considered to improve efficiency and effectiveness of governments. When the number and size of government administrations are reduced, there is a reduction in administrative costs. Why should citizens who live in a city pay more taxes to support the city's administration while the citizens who live in the unincorporated county have lower tax bills? The citizens receive the same services.

In the eighteenth century, there was a need to get the states to support the federal government. In the twenty-first century, the federal government should be organized to support the state governments.

Social borders and government borders exist for different reasons. According to the Declaration of Independence, the people form governments to support their "safety and happiness." Large or small governments do not necessarily bring about their desired purpose. It is up to the citizens and taxpayers to bring about governments that meet their goals.

CHAPTER 11

IT IS TIME FOR ACTION

BRING GOVERNMENT INTO THE TWENTY-FIRST CENTURY

The United States has been a leader and a role model for other nations. In the case of government, the United States and France were among the first nations to benefit from the Age of Enlightenment. While the citizens enjoyed individual freedom and the rewards of a republican form of government, the organization and formation of local governments followed what was present in Europe at the time of the monarchy.

Thus, we have county and local governments with both large and small populations. Like the rest of the world, there are too many governments in the United States. It is time for the United States to once again take its role as a world leader and reorganize the governments to improve effectiveness and especially efficiency.

President Clinton recognized the overgrowth of the federal government during his first administration. Clinton appointed

Al Gore to organize the federal government. While some slight progress was made, the task ended before the job was complete. Gore did manage to claim credit for the Internet. (LOL)

When there is a task as large as organizing all governments, it is a task for the best and brightest persons. They need to think outside the box. There needs to be a Constitutional Congress that consists of these members charged with proper reorganization of the federal government and organization of state, county, and local governments. With these members and a collective search for wisdom, there should be individual freedom and republic governments for all the nation's governments. The governments should be effective and efficient.

The advancement in the ability to store, retrieve, and work with data that occurred in the last half of the twentieth century will aid all governments. The continuing growth of this knowledge must be encouraged. The growth of technology that is seen in Silicon Valley must be supported with every effort.

Now for a very radical idea—should the federal government and California's government consider making the Silicon Valley area an international area? If this decision was made, would it encourage talented foreign citizens and foreign investments to come to the area? Having the development of technology so near would be a great advantage to the United States. While we have welcomed the poor and the tired, it is time that we welcomed the best and the brightest.

When the task of reorganizing the governments to promote effectiveness and efficiency is completed, the United States will once again show the leadership shown by the framers of the Constitution.

CHAPTER 12
THE AMERICAN DREAM

If the American Dream is to continue to exist, every member of society will have to make an effort to protect the Dream. The population growth in the United States and in the world has provided markets that support development. Will the rapid growth of the population outpace the rate of American job growth? Will the growth of the senior citizen population outpace the growth in health care and available finance? American citizens will be in competition with citizens of other nations in this century. The citizens will need to be equally or better prepared for the work force in this century. The American Dream requires rewards for work and accomplishments. Without the rewards the Dream will die.

The size of the United States leaves areas for growth and development. While most states are gaining population, a few states have lost population. Family farms are decreasing and agriculture has become a corporate industry. More people are moving to large metropolitan areas. There is not only a high rate of growth of these cities—there is the addition of population to the area outside the city limits.

The major metropolitan areas have large populations and, in most of the states, they represent more than half the population of the state. In fact, most of the population in the states is found in the areas around large cities. This population distribution helps increase the population served by a single government. This distribution also provides for reduction of the administrative costs for providing services. The number of governments and the size of the governments must be controlled by the taxpayers. These large population centers are served by a city council and a county government. The small populations in the other areas require the same government agencies. With control of these governments, there should be a decrease in administrative costs. There needs to be a reduction in all governments. For example, since the school board in the large population serves large numbers, why do we need so many school boards? The money saved could better be used in the classroom. Education is only one area where mergers of functions occur within the governments.

At the beginning of the twentieth century and the twenty-first century, we have seen depression or recession. After the Roaring Twenties in the twentieth century and the dot-com bubble in the late twentieth century, we have seen bubbles burst and recessions.

Families and government need to save in the good years because the good years do not last forever. The experiences of the past should teach citizens to not only live inside their income, but to live inside their income and their savings plan. The cost of the increasing senior population will reduce the ability of the government to provide support to these citizens.

Therefore, the working population in the twenty-first century will need to plan well for their retirement years.

Thinking outside the box also includes thinking into the future. For almost 250 years, citizens have lived the American Dream. The United States has been the land of opportunity.

Inside-the-box thinking by both governments and citizens will not keep the American Dream alive. At the start of the twentieth-first century, we are seeing large unemployment rolls. Both high school and college graduates will need to be educated to know how to find jobs.

Today, few high school or college graduates know the importance of their curriculum vitae. Building a proper CV begins with courses taken in high school and college. Having a job during school also provides valuable experience. The ever-increasing cost of education and the decrease in government funds will require students to become employed while they are in school.

The sooner students learn the value of developing an excellent CV and the value of networking to find a job, the better their chances are for finding good jobs after they complete their education.

It should be remembered that learning is a lifetime process. Internet search engines have improved the knowledge available to students who need jobs. Websites describe jobs, their rate of pay, and the knowledge and skills required to be considered for the job. The students need to use this information to improve their CV. The CV should include information about how the student's courses and experience fit the job description.

Parents, graduates, and governments support educational institutions. The government needs to take a greater notice of the support that educational institutions are giving to society.

Graduates know the problems they faced after they graduated and should make this knowledge known to their school, college, or university. Their government representatives need to be informed about educational problems. Feedback should bring about improvement.

Competition grows as the population grows. In order to meet the competition, students at all levels will need education that prepares them for the technology of the twenty-first century. It is easy for technology to outgrow education. Constant study and review of the curriculum is necessary. Everyone should ask if they are getting his or her money's worth.

The development of the electronic media has made it very easy for anyone to find information and gain knowledge. The cost of education—especially college and graduate school—is increasing at an alarming rate. The nation felt the results of the 1920s and the 1990s when the bubbles burst; people lost most of their material gains.

Are colleges and universities in for a similar fall? When governments and individuals perceive the effects of the electronic media and the Internet on teaching and learning, they will realize that it is time for major changes in the educational systems.

While the United States was leading the world in technology and economic growth, citizens were competing with the other Americans for jobs. In the twenty-first century, United States citizens will be competing with the world population, especially India and China. We have evidenced the growth of Japan since World War II. Every day we hear how American students are falling behind the students of other countries.

Einstein said, "Insanity is doing the same thing over and

over again and expecting different results." It is time to change the government's organization and methods.

After World War II, citizens had the opportunity to increase their standard of living, but the late twentieth century and the beginning of the twenty-first century have not provided the same opportunity. Many manufacturing jobs have been shipped to other countries where labor is less expensive.

This shipment of jobs to other countries has increase job opportunities in those countries and increased the total market. But, incomes in the United States have not increased at the same rate. Opportunity drives the economy. If the American economy is to grow at a rate near the rate of the population growth, the nation will have to learn to compete with other countries. Otherwise, opportunities will not be available and the economy will suffer.

The Soviet Union is a good example of opportunity and economy. With the communist government, opportunity was not available to the citizens and the economy failed. The citizens did not produce and the communist government went bankrupt. Capitalism must learn from the Soviet Union's experience.

Capitalism needs incentives for its citizens. When there are opportunities and rewards for work, it is human nature to want to work. Corporations that ship jobs to other countries need to remember this. Greed can kill the goose that is laying the golden eggs.

In the 1950s, "corporate conscience" was heard often. Labor unions had grown until corporate leadership had to recognize the power of the working population. Many corporations became worker-owned companies. As the corporation made more money, the workers benefited through their ownership of company stock.

During and after the Vietnam War, there was a lessening of the respect for employees and the society of the United States. "God is dead!" was heard frequently. While it may not make a difference whether you are a religious person are not, human values are necessary for the success of society.

The loss of corporate conscience has resulted in the move of jobs to other countries. There has been a major shift in net wealth among the various levels of society in the United States population. This loss of concern for our neighbors has resulted in a loss of opportunity for American citizens.

In the twenty-first century, United States citizens will be competing for jobs with the world's population. The United States will not be the world leader in manufacturing with jobs shipped to other countries. Hard work will not pay off for the citizens of the twenty-first century as it did for the citizens of the twentieth century.

All aspects of the society will be competing with the societies of the world. American society will need to work together. There will be a need for return to both individual and corporate conscience. The nation will need an educational system that supports the needs of society. Students will not be able to leave school without the knowledge and experience to compete for jobs.

The United States can still lead in technology development. But, this will take government programs like the ones used in the past to stimulate growth. The space program that was put in place by President Kennedy is a good example of government-led growth of necessary technology.

The president just stopped the space program to reduce government spending, but no program has been put in place to provide the technology growth produced by the space program.

Without growth in jobs and income opportunities, the citizens become complacent like the Soviet population. Do we want to go bankrupt—or do we want a government that thinks ahead?

A reduction in the size and cost of government can make money available for economic growth and citizens' opportunities. Only the same opportunities provided by capitalism in the past can keep the United States on track for success. It is time to think outside the box. One question that will have to be asked is: "Is the welfare of society better served when the citizens work for the improvement of the corporations and society, or is society better served by citizens who depend on a benevolent government?"

The American Dream can only exist as long as there is opportunity and rewards for work and success.

SUMMARY

The author has stressed the need for "collective search for wisdom" by all government legislatures. Individual fiat is frowned upon, but the author has practiced individual fiat throughout the book. It is impossible to have a collective search for wisdom between the author and the reader of a book. Feedback is appreciated.

While the estimate of the number of governments is low, eighteen thousand governments to provide services to just over three hundred million citizens is excessive and expensive. The current financial situation has caused some governments to decrease the size of their legislatures. Other areas need to follow their lead. Why do citizens and taxpayers in counties with populations less than one or two hundred thousand need additional, costly local governments? The county government should be organized to provide all the necessary services.

When several nearby counties have populations less than one to two hundred thousand, why don't they merge? The savings in tax dollars in administrative costs is necessary for programs and services during these periods of financial difficulty.

The federal budget and the deficit are good evidence that the government is dysfunctional and excessively expensive. Duplication of programs and government offices is obvious. The duplication results in duplication of responsibility and complicates decision making. The executive branch's answer to problems is to create another layer of government.

The author has attempted to point out that potential problems were recognized very early in the formation of the federal government. These warnings were ignored and, as a result, we have problems today. Elected officials have not taken the factors of time and population into their decisions. Government officials need to review the history before they enact new programs or laws.

With a government "of the people, by the people, for the people," it becomes necessary for voters and taxpayers to assume responsibility for the effectiveness of the government. All citizens—not just the vocal minority—need to be heard. When representatives are not responsive, they should be voted out of office. There is an old saying that citizens get the type of government they deserve.

It is time that citizens assume the responsibility and bring about mergers to decrease the administrative cost of government. Citizens need to organize and insist on a new constitutional convention charged with organizing all the governments—especially the federal government.

The twenty-first century will offer new technology and new experiences. It is up to the citizens to make the most of these advances. Knowing the history of good and bad experiences and heeding the advice given by the experiences of the past is important. The benefits that citizens can obtain can keep the American Dream alive and well. The nation should not have another experience like the recessions of the early twenty-first century. Every citizen should keep in mind Einstein's advice about insanity. It is time to change the government's organization and methods.

Organizing governments to improve function and efficiency calls for a collective search for wisdom by the best and the brightest.